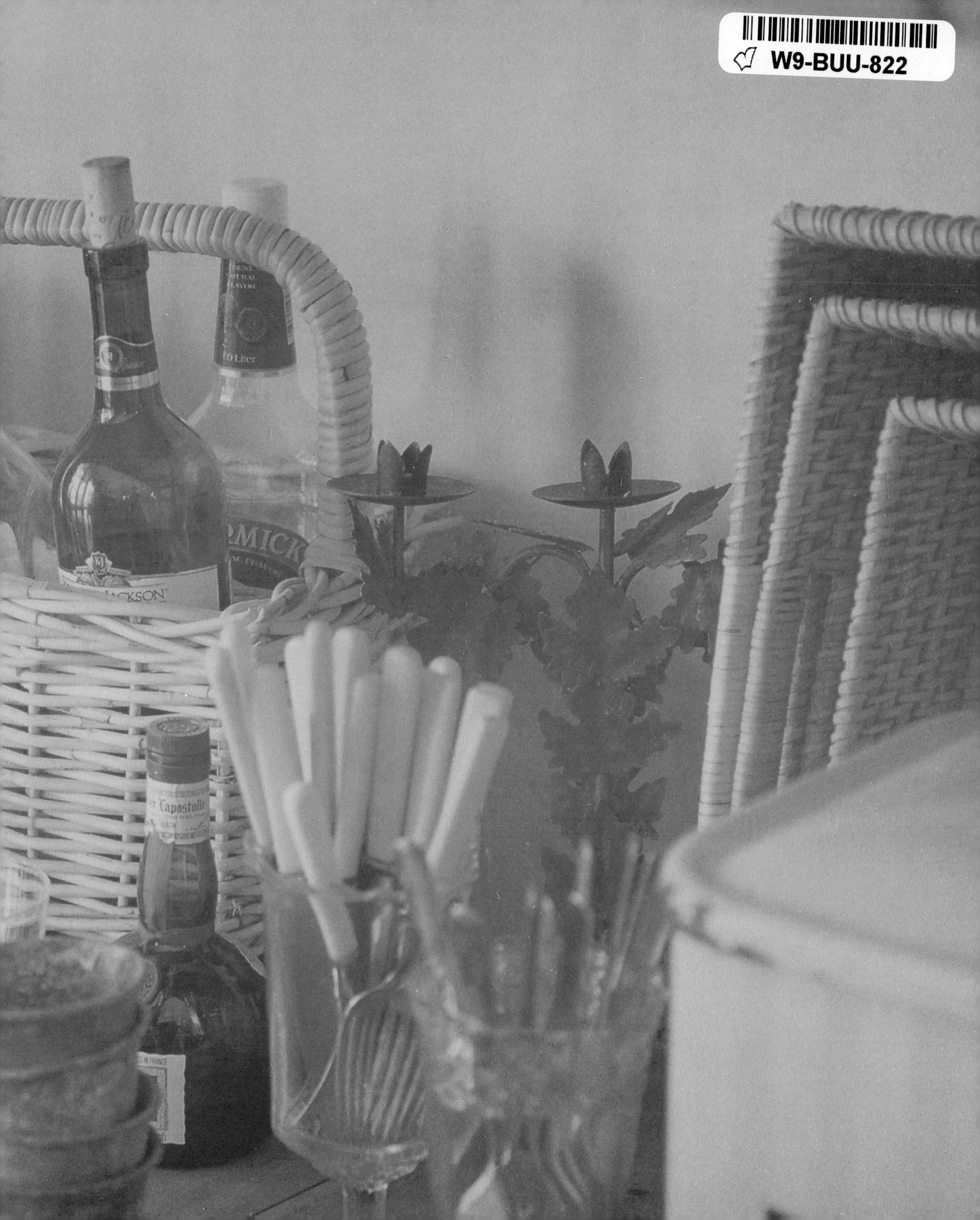

MODERN
COUNTRY

A vintage teak chaise from a cruise ship keeps company with a large wicker trunk in the back entry. The black-framed mirror reflects abundant light entering through the wall of glass. Texture and color come from the antique crazy quilt and kilim rug. A collection of ribbons won at horse shows across the country adds color without clutter.

SOUVENI

Color and pattern—

and a lot of it— may seem to contradict the "keep it simple" philosophy (facing). Collections, though, have been reduced and refined, leaving tables cleaner and less cluttered. An unpretentious painted-concrete floor and a tough sisal rug ground the collage. Between the wing-backed chairs sits an outdoor garden table. Assignments for furniture are as broad as your imagination. The classic metal floor lamp comes from a doctor's office.

Souvenirs and keepsakes are memory makers. Nothing is more nostalgic. A Statue of Liberty lamp (left) typifies the genre.

The FIRST CAFETERIAS
in JOPLIN MO., ST. JOSEPH MO.
TULSA OKLA., OKLAHOMA CITY
DALLAS TEX., HOUSTON TEX.
OPENED, OWNED *and* OPERATED *by*
(1916-'17-'18-'19)   *Stewart B. Ware*

CAMP
WENOKA

"Visitors welcome" could be the password to this free-spirited home (facing). Fascinated by the humor and graphics depicted in signs, the owner gravitates toward anything with words on it. The vintage Westinghouse fan, an old zinc lunch box and zinc cups holding sea biscuits from the beach bring modern into the mix.

In the family room (above left), signs discovered at yard sales and flea markets complement a vintage portrait—purchased because the subject reminded the homeowner of someone she knew—and an oil of "two old ladies holding pigs," painted by Montana artist Beth Loftin. The table's industrial iron base with added wood top showcases a miniature train station hand-made by a grandfather for his grandson.

Old group photographs known as "yard longs" become treasured finds (left). Although discovered at different times and in different places, the photos share an ironic connection. The creative homeowner named the grouping: "Brains" (SHS Graduating Class), "Beauty" (Miss America Pageant), "Sinners" (Erie, Pennsylvania Bartenders Picnic), and "Saints" (Women's Christian Temperance Movement).

Wall-to-wall books and a pair of turn-of-the-century chairs, discovered at the Paris flea market, create an intimate reading nook in what used to be an upstairs porch. The leather chairs look trendy refurbished with new cushions and an outline of fuzzy fringe. The S shape of the modern ottoman adds style and service.

chapter 2

Three centuries of design combine to create this setting. Vintage 1940s flea-market draperies and 1930s aluminum chairs, salvaged from a landmark hotel, mix with a nineteenth-century English farm table and a twenty-first-century Louis XV–style "ghost" chair by Philippe Starck (see page 41). Illumination comes from the industrial-style hanging light fixtures.

Dine IN
eclectic and
simple

Dining in is not all about food. Where you dine and the setting in which you enjoy food is as important as the food itself, be it gourmet or Chinese take-out. Whether the dining room is formal—complete with the traditional chandelier, hutch or Welsh dresser—or a cozy corner in the kitchen, the table is the centerpiece of this room's decorating theme. If the design theme is country, you can almost count on a harvest or farm table to be the dining room's gathering place. But if it's modern country, you have many varied options—and a design-conscious dining room is not afraid of an eclectic mix.

For a brilliant fusion of styles and periods, antique chairs can flank a sleek glass-topped table with chrome legs. Or just the opposite. In a stream-side cottage, Italian leather Cab chairs cozy up to an antique English double gate-leg table. Use a conventional farm table and surround it with a mix-match of modern, vintage or aluminum chairs. All provide a spirit of contrast and whimsy. No guests, in any of these settings, have been dismayed at the merging of periods and materials or inconvenienced at the unusual seating arrangements around the dining table. Instead, the element of surprise and contrast has drawn legions of praise for all of the homeowners.

On one dining table, a simple planter of growing grass makes a minimalist centerpiece. In another home, a sculptured horse from an old weather vane graces the

A prime example of melding old with new: an eighteenth-century-style Louis XV chair replicated in Lucite, a contemporary material that gives the chair its "ghostly" see-through appearance, presents the illusion of taking up less space than a conventional chair. A deliberate lack of clutter allows the different surfaces and materials to play their role.

center of the table. Gone, or at least put away (maybe even retired or given estate sale status), are crystal candlesticks, formal vases filled with flowers and ornate urns that have no relation to the current modern country design.

If dining room tables have taken on a new life, the conventional hutch or buffet is also enjoying double duty. While a hutch may house prized china, family heirlooms, or special collections of ironstone, it also plays a dual role by serving as a handmaiden to the bar, making entertaining much simpler.

One of the most obvious nods to the modern country theme is evidenced in the kind of lighting that now illuminates the dining area. Retired are the elaborate brass-and-crystal chandeliers that brought a formal elegance to dining and entertaining lifestyles of the past.

In one home, a straightforward black wrought-iron chandelier is slightly dressed up in red shades trimmed with beads. Even with the adornment, its simplicity remains intact. In another home, modern pendant lights illuminate the bar adjacent to an informal country dining area. Hovering over that centerpiece of planted grass, are two green-enamel industrial hanging light fixtures that blend perfectly with the green in the room's floral curtains.

Dining for the modern country crowd seems to be much more about personal pleasure and hosting your friends and family in a setting that is warm and comfortable, without any element of pretense.

In this revamped kitchen, simple Shaker-style cabinets—one with doors and one without—installed against a solid wall of glass, flood the space with natural light (facing). The pine cupboards act as a frame around the sink. A play of textures occurs with the stainless-steel countertop, reproduction farmhouse sink, shiny chrome fixtures and bright cabinet pulls. The island's concrete surface continues the mix and supports the unfitted style of a kitchen where not everything matches. The result is enlightening.

A Shaker-style pine cupboard (above) makes the perfect backdrop for a traditional pot rack showcasing colorful bowls.

You might call this kitchen "American Agrarian" to describe its transformation from the original 1968 pod-style architecture to the open, country design it is today (above). The farmhouse-style sink, big enough to wash large pans or small dogs, is by Kohler.

(Facing clockwise) "Kitchen Technician" is the term humorously assigned by the homeowner to the random red enamel letters she found at a flea market. Weighted iron with a milk glass shade makes up the reproduction light fixture. A big-number alarm clock plays a key role in the food prep area. A vintage rubber glove mold grasps a tea towel—and brings a smile. The old diner menus, also flea-market treasures, often inspire requests from friends: gizzards and livers for 85 cents is a favorite order.

FRENCH FRIES   .20
ONION RINGS   .35

DINNERS
GIZZARDS & LIVERS
Small CHICKEN Dinner   85
HAMBURG Steak   85
CHICKEN FRY Steak
Breaded PORK TENDER
FRIED HAM Dinner

"The whole is better than its parts," certainly describes the center island in this kitchen (facing). The custom piece, made by Tulsan Dale Gillman, consists of a chest of drawers, a coffee table and a pair of nightstands stacked back-to-back. A well-constructed platform and painted finish unite the disparate antique pieces. Plenty of storage abounds with the extensive number of shelves and drawers contained beneath the granite top. The vaulted ceiling, open shelving and painted surfaces add French flair to the country look. The shiny steel of a modern industrial range contrasts the classic influences.

A collection of brown-and-white transferware (above), carefully arranged and accessible on open shelving, adds classic beauty to this eclectic kitchen.

Translating
yesterday to today's

country style, this kitchen relies on antique and reproduction pieces to spell out a streamlined image. Old and new items that originated in a butcher shop prove graphic in their "wordy" presentation. Up-to-date appliances with sleek lines merge flawlessly into the fresh and time-less setting. In the mix, concrete countertops add heft and texture, while the painted cabinets reflect a light and airy spirit. An aged wire baker's stand displays a collection of wicker-wrapped bottles.

Say "cheese" (facing) brings a smile to a kitchen arrangement that mixes white pottery, concrete counters and a contemporary black lamp.

In a small kitchen without enough space on the countertop, a stainless-steel pot rack transforms into a shelf with room for a microwave, a topiary and china. Fenced in by an antique footed tray, glass and metal canisters disclose their contents for easy accessibility. A stovetop vignette typifies the idea to "Keep it simple and keep it clean, but spice it up with something unexpected."

In this chef's kitchen, the hardworking commercial range creates a picture of modern utility (facing) when paired with reclaimed tin ceiling tiles. The pressed ceiling tiles, sandblasted and powder coated a glossy black, insure easy upkeep. An old factory clock, found in England at the Newark Antique Fair, adds to the industrial-meets-retro mix and perfectly depicts modern country style.

A wall of glass bricks illuminates an old shoe-drying rack (above left) enlisted into service for china storage. The bricks add subtle texture with their carefully chosen variety of alternating patterns.

Minimal by its lack of color, the all-white china makes a generous impact (above right and facing).

The sculptural lines of antique clothes hangers (facing top left) offset the graphic form of an obsolete industrial wooden gear.

The number *three* intrigues decorators and photo stylists. There's something about the balance of three that lends itself to an interesting arrangement, like a trio of old clocks looking just right lined up by height on a wall shelf (facing bottom left).

Coat and *walk*—more words in a humorous collection of elementary flash cards (facing right) go with a practical wall hanger.

Inspiration for this reproduction demilune table came from an authentic seventeenth-century one (below). A trio of white and yellow antique bowls stands out against the contrast of the dark wood. In case you don't recognize the hats, an old elementary flash card will jog your memory. Words add a graphic element to almost any arrangement.

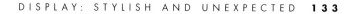

A wall of
bookcases, salvaged from a kitchen-

remodeling project and transferred to the family room, supports books, photographs and an entertainment center (facing). Notice how the shelves look balanced with different heights and textures. Painting the walls an edgy gold adds dimension.

Grouping like items together makes a dramatic statement. A wall of pictures will present a more cohesive whole if the individual pictures have something in common, such as this collection of landscape paintings (above). This can also be accomplished with a collection of black-and-white photographs with identical frames, or mismatched frames all in the same color.

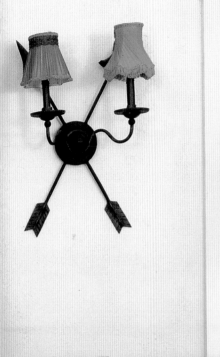

The reproduction pine hutch displays a grand collection of quills, bone beakers, old silver, books and antique English tea caddies (facing). The similar color of all the objects keeps the arrangement in check. A pair of iron sconces adds symmetry on either side of the hutch.

Trays of all kinds, whether silver or wicker, footed or not, contain disparate items and present them as one (left). Used on tabletops or ottomans, the trays form a base for a collection that might otherwise lack cohesiveness.

In the 1930s and 1940s, manufacturers packaged cookies and various food items in tin boxes stamped to resemble wicker picnic baskets. These decorative yet practical items offer no end to storage and display possibilities. For added efficiency, label the contents with tags from an office supply store.

A screen constructed of faded, multicolored shutters does double duty as a room divider and photo gallery (facing). Made up of five six-foot-tall louvered wood shutters and held together by three sets of two-way folding hinges, the screen provides a division from a home office on the other side of the bedroom. Several white chip clips—from a delicatessen—display family snapshots. The design of the rod allows the clips and photos to simply hang over the top or in between the slats of the shutters.

Clips and magnets make it so family photos (left top and bottom), can show up everywhere on anything.

A collection of antique French ivory picture frames illustrates the idea that a grouping of similar items makes a bigger impact (below). The display includes clocks and dresser accessories also in French ivory.

A collection of Bakelite flatware shows off its colors in a ceramic flowerpot. The bright handles look as perky as a bouquet of zinnias (left).

Fashioned after a vintage milk bottle carrier, a new shiny steel adaptation can take on many chores. This one showcases colorful flatware ready for the next dinner party (right).

For innovative display and storage ideas, simply give useful objects new assignments. Old gym baskets make hip storage bins with their open wire framework (facing). No longer relegated to the gym, they can show up in every room of the house, whether displaying glasses, cups, bowls or towels.

The ingenious design of a stainless steel dish drainer hung on the wall above the sink allows it to drain, store and display dishes all at the same time (right).

ANTIQUE AND TRADITIONAL

Antique Hardware and Home
19 Buckingham Plantation Drive
Bluffton, SC 29910
800.422.9982
www.antiquehardware.com
Antique hardware and fixtures

Antique Warehouse
Dale Gillman
2406 E. 12th Street
Tulsa, OK 74104
918.592.2900
*Antique furniture, accessories and
light fixtures*

Beaver Creek Antiques Market
20202 National Pike
Hagerstown, MD 21740
301.739.8075
www.beavercreekantiques.com
*One-hundred-fifty dealers of antiques
and accessories*

Charles Faudree
1345 E. 15th Street
Tulsa, OK 74120
918.747.9706
www.charlesfaudree.com
Antiques and accessories

Country Garden Antiques
147 Parkhouse
Dallas, TX 75207
214.741.9331
Shabby antiques

Denver Antique Market
1298 S. Broadway
Denver, CO 80210
303.744.0281
Twenty dealers, all antique inventory

Legacy Trading Co.
3699 McKinney Avenue
Dallas, TX 75204
214.953.2222
Unique home furnishings and designs

T.A. Lorton
1343 E. 15th Street
Tulsa, OK 74120
918.743.1600
www.talorton.com
*Traditional and modern accessories,
lamps and fine linens*

The Shelby Mercantile
5072 Voelkel Road
Fayetteville, TX 78940
214.244.2814
theshelbyinn@aol.com
Country antiques and collectibles

Uncommon Objects
1512 S. Congress Avenue
Austin, TX 78704
512.442.4000
www.UncommonObjects.com
Eighteen purveyors of curious goods

The ingenious design of a stainless steel dish drainer hung on the wall above the sink allows it to drain, store and display dishes all at the same time (right).

ANTIQUE AND TRADITIONAL

Antique Hardware and Home
19 Buckingham Plantation Drive
Bluffton, SC 29910
800.422.9982
www.antiquehardware.com
Antique hardware and fixtures

Antique Warehouse
Dale Gillman
2406 E. 12th Street
Tulsa, OK 74104
918.592.2900
Antique furniture, accessories and light fixtures

Beaver Creek Antiques Market
20202 National Pike
Hagerstown, MD 21740
301.739.8075
www.beavercreekantiques.com
One-hundred-fifty dealers of antiques and accessories

Charles Faudree
1345 E. 15th Street
Tulsa, OK 74120
918.747.9706
www.charlesfaudree.com
Antiques and accessories

Country Garden Antiques
147 Parkhouse
Dallas, TX 75207
214.741.9331
Shabby antiques

Denver Antique Market
1298 S. Broadway
Denver, CO 80210
303.744.0281
Twenty dealers, all antique inventory

Legacy Trading Co.
3699 McKinney Avenue
Dallas, TX 75204
214.953.2222
Unique home furnishings and designs

T.A. Lorton
1343 E. 15th Street
Tulsa, OK 74120
918.743.1600
www.talorton.com
Traditional and modern accessories, lamps and fine linens

The Shelby Mercantile
5072 Voelkel Road
Fayetteville, TX 78940
214.244.2814
theshelbyinn@aol.com
Country antiques and collectibles

Uncommon Objects
1512 S. Congress Avenue
Austin, TX 78704
512.442.4000
www.UncommonObjects.com
Eighteen purveyors of curious goods

Shopping INspirations

MODERN AND CONTEMPORARY

Eurway
Texas stores in Austin, Dallas,
Houston (Call toll free for locations
877.9eurway)
www.eurway.com
International contemporary design

Hawley Design Furnishings
702 S. Utica Avenue
Tulsa, OK 74104
918.587.0510
Custom contemporary furnishings

Modern Furniture OKC
8913 North Western Avenue
Oklahoma City, OK 73114
www.modernfurnitureokc.com
*Furniture, lighting, accessories, 1950s
through 1970s*

Modernica
7366 Beverly Boulevard
Los Angeles, CA 90036
323.933.0383
www.modernica.net
Furnishings from midcentury designers

Richard Neel Interiors
3742 S. Peoria
Tulsa, OK 74105
918.742.4777

Retromodern.com
805 Peachtree Street
Atlanta, GA 30308
877.724.0093
www.retromodern.com
Modern designs for the home

S.R. Hughes
3410 S. Peoria
Tulsa, OK 74105
918.742.5515
www.srhughes.com
*Modern furnishings and contempo-
rary lighting*

Urban Furnishings
3638 S. Peoria
Tulsa, OK 74105
918.747.0510
*Contemporary furniture, lighting and
accessories*

ARCHITECTURAL SALVAGE

Architectural Accents
2711 Piedmont Road N.E.
Atlanta, GA 30305
404.266.8700
www.architecturalaccents.com

Architectural Antiques
1900 Linwood Avenue
Oklahoma City, OK 73109
405.232.0759

Old Theatre Architectural Salvage
2045 Broadway
Kansas City, MO 64108
816.283.3740
rick@architecturalsalvage.com

The Architectural Bank
1824 Filicity
New Orleans, LA 70113
504.523.2702

ANTIQUES FAIRS

Brimfield Antique Show
Route 20
Brimfield, MA 01010
www.brimfieldshow.com
One week, May, July, September

Newark International Antiques and Collectors Fair
Newark and Nottinghamshire
Showground
Nottinghamshire, England
www.dmgantiquefairs.com
*February, April, June, August,
October, December*

Round Top Antiques Fair
475 N. Hwy 237
Round Top, TX 78954
512.237.4747
www.roundtopantiquesfair.com
First weekend, April and October

Round Top Art Fair and Creative Market
1235 N. Hwy 237
Round Top, TX 78954
281.493.5501
turnyshows@aol.com
First weekend, April and October

Shelby Antique Show
Harmonie Hall
Shelby, TX 78940
281.373.9977
First weekend, April and October

The Annex Antique Fair and Flea Market
110 W. 19th Street
New York, NY 10011
212.243.5343
Saturday and Sunday, year-round

Warrenton Antique Fair
Warrenton Grocery Store
4309 S. State Hwy 237
Warrenton, TX 78961
979.249.3144
www.warrentontx.com
First weekend, April and October

FLEA MARKETS

Kane County Flea Market
Kane County Fairgrounds
St. Charles, IL
630.377.2252
First Sunday of month

Paris Flea Market
Paris, France
0892.705.765
www.Parispuces.com
Daily, year-round

Tulsa Flea Market
Tulsa Fairground
21st and Yale Avenue
Tulsa, OK
918.744.1113
Saturdays, 8 a.m. to 5 p.m.

Wichita Flea Market
Kansas Coliseum
N. 85th St. & I-135
Wichita, KS
620.663.5626
Third Sunday of month